Toy Guns

To Marilyn with appreciation
Mirella C. van der Zyl

Toy Guns

Childhood memories of war

MIRELLA COACCI VAN DER ZYL

authorHOUSE®

AuthorHouse™ LLC
1663 Liberty Drive
Bloomington, IN 47403
www.authorhouse.com
Phone: 1-800-839-8640

© 2014 Mirella Coacci van der Zyl. All rights reserved.

No part of this book may be reproduced, stored in a retrieval system, or transmitted by any means without the written permission of the author.

Published by AuthorHouse 07/24/2014

ISBN: 978-1-4969-1632-7 (sc)
ISBN: 978-1-4969-1631-0 (e)

Any people depicted in stock imagery provided by Thinkstock are models, and such images are being used for illustrative purposes only. Certain stock imagery © Thinkstock.

This book is printed on acid-free paper.

Because of the dynamic nature of the Internet, any web addresses or links contained in this book may have changed since publication and may no longer be valid. The views expressed in this work are solely those of the author and do not necessarily reflect the views of the publisher, and the publisher hereby disclaims any responsibility for them.

Contents

Acknowledgments ix
Introduction xi
Indonesia: Ernest 1
Italy: Mirella 12
Milano: Marina and Eugenio 30
Belgium: Noel 33
Canada: Libby 39
Canada: Jean 42
Canada: Bob 44
England: Margaret 46
England: Mary 50
England: Ted 53
England: Pat 55
France: Michelle 57
France, Normandy, and Belgium: Chet 60
Germany: Horst 63
Holland: Rita and Ton 68
Holland: Betty 72
Holland: Sylvia 76

Java: Theo	79
Java: Dan	82
Scotland: Lin	84
Singapore and Holland: Nellie	86
Uganda: Rick	90
Vietnam: Bill	94
Vietnam: Kim	96
Epilogue: The War within Ourselves	100

To my grandchildren, who are innocent of war.

Acknowledgments

My sincere appreciation to all those friends and family members I interviewed who contributed so much to the writing of this book. Without their memories to keep these stories alive and precious, we would not have this book.

My deepest gratitude to my dear son, Willem, who, in spite of being occupied with work and theater, edited my first draft of the book. My heartfelt thanks to Giselle and John, who coached my grandson, Hunter, to pose for the cover image. Thank you to my husband, Ernest, and my friends Gary Chalk and Libby for their advice and feedback. So many minds were at work in putting together these memories.

Introduction

I looked closely at the photo looming from the newspaper on the table. A small child was holding a gun, bigger than him, and the caption underneath said that a four-year-old boy was fighting alongside his companions.

I was stunned; a four-year-old should be holding a toy, a ball, a puppet—not a machine gun. What was going through his young mind? What did he understand of what was happening beyond the barricade behind which he stood?

At times, on TV news we see groups of people fighting in the streets and throwing grenades, and there are always children running with them, participating in the violence.

These are children who should be at home with their parents, in school, or playing outside with their friends. What goes on in their minds when they take part in those fights, when they follow soldiers, guerrillas, or demonstrators? Do they understand the purpose of those wars? Or do they just follow blindly because it is exciting and makes them feel grown up?

The image of the boy and all the questions it raised rekindled memories of the years of war in Italy, where I was born and grew up, and prompted me to write about the impact war has on children. Adults see war as their only means to defend their beliefs, to fight for freedom from dictators, or to free their country from unwanted people. Are they fully aware of the damage these conflicts inflict on the lives of their children, besides the lack of food and shelter? Do they consider the impact on children's sense of security or future stability?

Streams of memories rush through my mind of the war times in Italy; these memories will be in my life forever. These experiences have shaped my life in ways both good and bad.

For example, I shudder at the waste of food I see in homes, restaurants, and conferences. When I see plates half full of perfectly good food tossed in the garbage, memories of days with little food, saved and scraped, come to my mind.

Toy Guns

When I hear sirens, the loud noise of an aircraft, or explosions, I am still shaken to the core remembering the alarms and the bombardments in my early years.

Over the years, I have heard many stories of war from people who lived through it. Here is one from my friend Paolo:

He was eight years old when the war came to his small village near Campobasso, South of Napoli. He remembers the terror of the bombing near his house. Screaming, he ran down into the basement while walls, the roof, and pavement crumbled around him. He must have passed out, because when he opened his eyes, everything was dark, and for a while he did not know where he was. Slowly he got up and recognized the basement, now full of rubble. He did not know what had happened to his family upstairs.

He peered through a hole in the basement walls that were still standing and saw his street littered with rubble and people screaming. As he watched, the steeple of the church crumbled and fell before his eyes. Soldiers stomped through the street shouting orders, filling Paolo with fear.

A truck arrived, full of men, and many women ran after it, crying. He thought he saw his mother but was not sure. The women were calling the names of their sons and husbands and trying to get them down from the truck. A shooting of artillery pushed some of the women to the ground, unmoving, and Paolo realized they had been shot dead.

He retreated into the darkness of the basement and thought about what to do. After sundown, he would go to what remained of the church, where he had seen people going, mostly women and children, to look for his family.

He looked again through the hole and saw someone wearing boots standing close to his house. Paolo hid in the darkness, under planks nearby, and waited, his heart beating in his throat. The boots stopped at the front of the house, and Paolo heard someone speaking in a strange language. What would happen if they found him?

Paolo suddenly felt very thirsty and hot, and, to his chagrin, he wet his pants. He waited, hardly breathing. The boots slowly turned away, and there was silence around him. Paolo waited for a while still. Then, slowly, he looked for the small sink in the basement and also for some of the food his mother had stored. He found vegetables under some planks. They were covered with dust and debris, but he ate them all the same.

Paolo tried to move some wood and planks that were blocking a door leading outside. With much struggle, he managed to make a hole big enough to squeeze himself through and saw a gutter still standing against a piece of wall. Water leaked from the gutter, and he drank it.

Returning to the basement and the hole he had made in the wall of debris, he looked outside. It was getting dark, and he decided to sleep for a while and then attempt to go to the bombarded church.

When he woke up, it was very dark, and he slipped out of his house, hiding in the darkness of some houses still standing. Little by little, he gained ground to the church and entered it by way of a few broken steps. There were many people sleeping on the floor, and he recognized one of the priests near a fire cracking in a small gas tank. Gladly, he ran to the priest, who embraced him. The priest took Paolo to a group of people nearby, and there Paolo saw his mother and two sisters, who screamed with joy at seeing him. They had thought him dead

All together now, the family decided to walk to Paolo's uncle's farm near the village and stay with him until the end of the war. Paolo's father had been taken by the SS to be sent to the front in Germany, and they had no other family nearby. And so they did, and there they found a life of relative peace and safety with their uncle and his family until the end of the war. However, Paolo's father never came back, and so Paolo took on the role of man of the household, looking after his family until they came to Canada after the war.

These are the kinds of stories in this book, which I wrote after interviewing several friends and relatives. Their memories, and my own, are still vivid and painful.

The cover photo is of my mother-in-law, Gerda Jansen, and her son, Ernest, my husband. They are attending a meeting called a Kumpulan in Mississauga. It is a meeting of prisoners of war from Indonesia, and most of them are Dutch people of about the same age and circumstances. Many survived the horror of prison camps and are still here, on earth today, where they meet a few times a year.

Gerda and Ernest are survivors of the concentration camp in Indonesia. Ernest was just a small boy of three. From their stories, which they remember in great detail, it is apparent that those years had a profound impact on their lives. Even today I see the effects of prison in their frugality, misery, bitterness about life, fear for the future, and pessimism about the world.

As I listened to the stories of many people my age, I realized how memories of war stay with us forever. They never change or fade away, and they influence our lives irreversibly. To illustrate war's impact, I have gathered memories of people from different countries that went through the war at a young age. These stories are meant as a warning of war's lasting negative effects on people's lives. Perhaps there is a chance that our young people, reading these stories, may learn to avoid war at all costs and, instead, grow strong in their faith, honesty, and the building up of their country.

Indonesia: Ernest

In 1939 Europe was going up in flames. At the time, my family was in Indonesia, West Java, and was going through hard times, even before the onslaught of the war reached us. My father had difficulty keeping a job, and my mother was at home with me, an infant. Father and Mother decided to divorce, and he joined the Dutch Army.

There was no work for white women outside the home, not even on the plantation where we resided. Secretarial work was done by educated local people. Despite being a fully qualified nurse, there was no work for my mother.

Rumors and sketchy news from the Netherlands, our homeland, about the war there disturbed us deeply. In May 1940 the Netherlands capitulated to Germany, after four days of violent fighting. Closer to home, the Japanese attacked Pearl Harbor in December 1941, and the United States declared war on the Japanese. During the ensuing months, the Allies lost every single battle with the Japanese. My family was fearful of what was happening.

My mother married a close friend of my father's. Her new husband worked on the tea plantation.

My stepfather was betrayed by the plantation administrator for destroying the gasoline supply, as his government had ordered him—and others unsympathetic to the Japanese—to do. He was imprisoned, tortured, and interrogated.

The most traumatic event for me at this time was impaling my toes on the garden rake. I was almost two, and I still remember how it hurt.

During my stepfather's absence, almost everyone on the estate made sure that Mother was provided with adequate food.

By then I had a little brother, Nick, and stayed with mother on the estate, fed by the locals who came daily with food. Mother got along well with these people because she knew the language and worked hard to be their friend. For example, before the war, one man was so devoted to her that he bought, at his own expense, several orchid plants and transported them on top of a bus to our home, where he planted a lovely garden for her.

Eventually the Japanese came to our plantation, and we were told to pack a suitcase, a plate a cup, cutlery and a potty which were suspended from a belt around mother's waist, and to walk a distance of seventeen kilometers to the city of Bandung. Two days later we were transferred via train to Bandung, which was, coincidentally, my birthplace. My stepfather was put on a boat and sent to Burma to work on the railroad. In Bandung the climate was pleasant, fortunately, as our stay lasted two years. We were in a large room in a house with other people, notably the wife of an army soldier who was not very pleasant. We were assigned to houses furnished by the Chinese. Our area in Bandung was called Karees.

Mother managed to find some work, mainly doing laundry and ironing. Ironing was done with cast irons filled with coals. with the money she earned and knowing the Sundanese language, she was able to carry on clandestine trade with the locals for fruit, vegetables, eggs, and also a kind of cereal, called sago, that made a good porridge that we had daily and shared with a sister of the Roman Catholic order. Mother also smuggled bread in baskets that had, at one time, contained manure.

We had our humorous moments. Mother had been away to deliver laundry. Nick somehow managed to get to a basket of twenty-nine eggs, smashing every one. He was found fast asleep with half an eggshell perched on his nose.

In Bandung, Nick became severely ill with dysentery, from which he later recovered. The Japanese, in their wisdom, decided to put all of us on a train, the trip lasting one full night. Nick was running a high fever, and I was left to fend for myself at the age of four.

We arrived at Batavia, now Jakarta, at sunrise. Women and children were physically and unceremoniously escorted to waiting trucks and manhandled aboard the vehicles. A short ride brought us to our new abode. Mother had been sitting on the knitting needles of a fellow passenger. Nick was immediately taken to the hospital.

Our new accommodations were far more crowded and far less pleasant than in Bandung. For the first few nights, we slept on the bare stone floor, our mattresses still in Bandung. After several moves, the remaining years in captivity were spent in a large room with only one window and one door leading to what we would today call sanitary facilities. There were no screens on the points of access, no mosquito netting, and eleven of us slept on mattresses and one field cot, all infested with bed bugs. Mother had to go to the hospital with dysentery, leaving me temporarily as an orphan being looked after by strangers. Nick went back to the hospital on his fourth birthday and died a week and a half later. The medical staff, made up mostly of nurses, in addition to their regular work, arranged for funeral services, which was really just a disposal of the body. There was no ceremony, and mother and Ernest left the hospital soon after. My mother had some measure of closure, though; Nick was no longer suffering.

As we were trudging home, mother moved slowly. She had severe edema in her legs. Suddenly we heard the sound of bugles blown by two Japanese soldiers, and the camp doors opened. At that signal, we knew we had to get off the street as quickly as possible. We made it just in time.

Food was doled out to us. It was not nearly as appetizing or nutritious as what we had in Bandung. As in Bandung, our camp of ten thousand people in Tjideng, the largest in Java, had a daily assembly, the *kumpulan*.

During a period of three days, we had no food.

In Bandung, after the daily appearance of the camp commander, who roared in on his motorcycle, we were usually left alone. In Tjideng, after some sort of roll call, we had to stand at attention in precise and rigid patterns for hours. Every so often, we had to bow and call out in Japanese, as dictated by the soldiers who yelled out these commands.

It was very hot, the country being in the tropics, 15 degrees south of the equator. Many people had no footwear and had to stand barefoot on the scalding hot pavement. Mother always tried to stand near the back of the assembly so she would not be noticed much and I could surreptitiously sit down on her feet.

People in the camp were often very sick with dysentery, diphtheria, and malaria. Strangely, I was not affected by these sicknesses; I did not even get the mumps. Water was severely rationed—no more than a few liters per day for the entire household of eleven people.

Open fires were not allowed. Once a ranking Japanese soldier rushed through the house with a cup of water and unceremoniously poured it on the fire someone had managed to start.

Once a month, the camp commander, known as Sonei, took it in his head that the entire camp population should be roused out of their beds to walk the streets at night. Fortunately the moon was full, because there was a danger of falling into an open sewer hole. All the grates were removed to make the sewers easier to pump out after we had completed the daily task of emptying the pots that were our toilets. By morning we were in an unfamiliar neighborhood, entering houses vacated by people who, like us, were temporarily nomads in the city. After a few hours, we would manage to struggle back to our abode.

During our stay, there were rumors about the status of the war. However, I am not clear when we were liberated. It happened sometime after the middle of August 1945.

On August 15, the Japanese surrendered, but our liberation didn't start until well into September, because the Allies could not get to the prisoners fast enough. A British Indian soldier was standing beside a large cargo truck called a fifteen hundred weight. He had a smile on his face, a turban on his head, a beard and moustache, and so we assumed we were free. Ironically, a few Japanese soldiers were told to guard us against the habitant of the village who were on a rampage, killing people and smashing everything in sight.

These rampages lasted for an undetermined period of time, but we were fed with bread, again delivered in baskets that also delivered manure. We also received another precious commodity: cigarettes. Finally we were evacuated by a British aircraft carrier, the HMS *Colossus*. We made the trip from Batavia to Ceylon in five days, a record, going around the west coast of Sumatra for fear of sea mines. We slept in airplane hangars below deck. To go on deck, we rode the aircraft elevator up. Food was excellent, and we were entertained by British sailors, who played field hockey on deck using triangular wooden pucks. On several occasions, Mother was hit in the ankles by the pucks.

On arrival in Ceylon, we were assigned to large wooden barracks that housed between fifty and seventy-five people each. Again the food was first rate, served in a communal dining hall. Our stay in Ceylon, now Sri Lanka, was approximately six months. On board the ship and in Ceylon, I learned my first English words and was treated to all sorts of new sights, like elephants working in the bush.

Finally the authorities managed to organize a transport, which consisted of a dilapidated ocean-going freighter taking on more people than its official capacity. On it, we set sail for Holland. The ship was so old and mechanically unsound that many times we would wake up not moving because of engine trouble. Mother was conscripted to organize entertainment for the several hundred children on board. Many times the upper deck was so hot that we could not walk there since we were barefoot. Every so often the sailors had to hose down the decks with sea water.

Mercifully, we finally managed to go through the Red Sea and the Mediterranean into the Atlantic Ocean, through the Gulf of Bisque, which happened to be storm free. We finally landed in Rotterdam, Holland, and we were taken by bus to Hilversum, where my aunt and her friend lived and took us in.

While we were interned in POW camps, there was an elaborate underground resistance movement by the Dutch people and a few native Indonesian Ambonese who happened to be loyal. These men spent their time engaged in sabotage wherever they found it expedient.

My father was in the army. He was eventually taken to prison, where he died. My stepfather was also taken prisoner and, after being tortured but not giving any information, was deported to Burma, where he worked on the famous railroad.

As a child I learned to conserve. If something broke, you fixed it or did without it. To this day I go through procedures and take actions that seem ridiculously miserly. We thought the existence we had would go on forever. There were constant rumors of victory and defeat. The boredom of our lives was only relieved by rumors, or real news, of raids by the Japanese soldiers. They committed atrocities in response to catching prisoners doing something contrary to rules, written and unwritten, such as trading with the locals. One commander took a bicycle chain and whipped people so caught.

The Japanese had their version of the Gestapo, called Kampitei, the secret police.

In the camps, we were bored, anxious and restless. There was not much to do. My mother kept alive the memories of her dead son Nick, and she was very uncertain about our future, especially for me, if something happened to her. The impact of the war has been strong on us, and we recounted many times the stories of our odyssey in Indonesia.

Because of the war, my education suffered and I was a poor student. I also had a condition with my thyroid and did not have medication un til much later. When I took the right medication, my grades in school improved greatly.

When we finally landed in Canada, we settled in Nova Scotia where, for many years we enjoyed a healthier and happier life.

Italy: Mirella

We did not suffer much hunger during the war, except for a few times that I remember. Even though I was only four, I did not ask my mother for food, because I sensed that if she could, she would have given it to me. She could always make lunches and supper with the little she had; she was resourceful and an excellent cook.

In those times, I had discovered a piece of wood that tasted really good when wet with water. So, when I felt hungry and knew I could not get any food, I would soak it in water, suck on it, and feel content.

I had noticed that the cupboard where my mother kept staples was gradually getting empty. There were just a few dried peas; some pasta; a little bit of flour, which my mother used to make wonderful pancakes for us; and a few other small packages, and I wondered why she did not refill them. I thought that perhaps she could not go out in the frigid weather we were experiencing that winter of 1945 or that she could not leave my newborn sister, Paola, at home.

One evening a group of partisans came to the door to ask for money or food to support them. The partisans were Italians who fought the Germans through the Resistance and lived in hiding in the mountains. My mother gave them a small bundle of pasta. Later on that night, I heard her cry with my father and tell him that she was running out of formula for my little sister and did not know what to do. She had always been unable to nurse us, in spite of all her efforts; her body just could not produce milk.

My father took her tenderly in his arms and let her cry. In that moment I sensed great despair and helplessness, and I knew it was because of the war. Everything bad that we experienced was because of it, and I was looking for a bright future without it. I had never experienced life yet without war.

After supper, when I was getting ready for bed, my mother sat at the kitchen table, her hands clasped, her head down. I knew she was praying.

In the morning, when the mail arrived, there was a postal money order from her well-to-do uncle. I do not remember if it was a gift for her birthday or for Christmas. Her uncle did that often with her, his favorite niece.

When I think back now, I wonder whether it was a coincidence, as many people would think, or God's providence for his children. I believe God is in the midst of war, providing and protecting his children in many ways. Because of my faith in him, I tend to believe that it was God's providence to all of us, at the right time

The war became so dangerous that my family fled to the mountains, to a small village called St. Antonino di Susa, where my uncle was the pastor of a small Baptist church. There was an apartment above the church, and he and his family lived on one side, while we lived in two small rooms on the other. A large kitchen connected the two rooms.

There was also a dark attic where my uncle stored many things. Once, my uncle and my dad hid there when the SS were looking for men to send to the front in Germany. They were not cowards, but, like many other Italians, they did not support the war into which Mussolini had led Italy.

My mother sent me to the attic several times when I was being particularly difficult. While I was afraid of the dark, there were empty jars that attracted me, and I would play with them. I would then ask the bad devil to get away from me, because I wanted to be a good little girl for my mom.

Often we heard the alarm sound in the village, and then planes would rumble over us. We would hear bombs explode not too far off. My sister Lidia and I would run out of the house, screaming in terror, and one time we saw a plane hovering close to us and heard its guns. My mother tried to follow us, but she was hindered by the fact that she was pregnant with my sister Paola and could not run after us. She yelled, "Throw yourself in the ditch." We did, running wildly, and until this day I do not know how we were spared from the fire of that plane.

The alarm would sound at the most inappropriate times, wrecking our lives and filling us with terror. To this day, the sound of a siren raises the hair on the back of my neck, and I am filled with a sense of dread. I think that sensation will be with me all my life.

One bright Sunday morning in spring, my sister Lidia was in a small tub having her bath, and I was playing with my dolls on the landing of the balcony.

The alarm sounded, dreadful and threatening. People had come to the church for the service, prepared to go on a picnic afterward. Quickly, my parents gathered us, and, in his haste, my father capsized my basket of dolls, to my great distress. I managed to grab one of them. My mother wrapped my sister in towels, grabbed clothes, bags of food, and blankets, and we all ran downstairs.

We joined the people of the church, who were already rushing to the mountains nearby. We walked to those mountains, where we hoped we would be safe as the planes bombarded residences and bridges.

The people slowly formed a line, climbing higher and higher up the mountain. I was sitting on my father's shoulders and heard singing: "In Alto, sopra I monti, press il cielo ognor vivro," the equivalent of the English hymn "I dwell in Beulah land."

Calm overtook us, and we reached a shady summit where people made themselves comfortable under the trees. My favorite playmate, Fido, a dog from one of the neighboring farms, came to me. I felt content sitting with my parents among our congregation.

My uncle led a brief service in the open air, and we sang several comforting hymns and prayed to our heavenly father to guard us and keep us safe.

Then we shared food we had brought with us. My father had lovely chocolate bars he got from the FIAT company, where he worked, and shared them with us. People put fruit and drinks in a nearby stream to keep them cool and shared lovely homemade bread, cheese, and salami made on the farms.

I felt safe there in the mountains, knowing that our Lord was looking at us from the clouds above. It was a beginning of a faith that has supported me since, through many difficult events in my life.

Up on the mountains, in the small village of St. Antonino, life was calmer than in Torino, and we ate better because the farmers grew their own food. I remember my mother buying a lot of fruit at a very small price and putting it on a large dresser. I used to take one piece of fruit for a snack and enjoy it. We had local jams on fresh bread and milk for breakfast.

My mother took us shopping in the village, and I still remember some of the places. At the end of the village, in the distance, there were domes and buildings shining in the sun. I used to think that it was where Santa Claus and God lived and was always dreaming of going there to visit one day.

Across the street from us, one neighbor was a widow who worked in a beautiful garden. She had a lot of white roses that smelled of a lovely fragrance. There was also a marmalade cat that did not like me and ran away as soon as it saw me.

On the corner there was a central store where you could buy just about anything. On a top shelf there were some beautiful dolls on display. I wanted so much to have one of them. Lidia and I talked about those dolls as if they were ours. We asked my mother if we could have them if we were very good. She always said that when the Allies came, we would be able to have them.

Everything good for me began to center on "when the Allies came." I did not know who they were, but to me they were like angels, because when they came, they would bring us dolls and many other good things.

Not everything was idyllic in our village. War was felt by everyone. Many of the men were gone. One lady who had a farm we visited often had gone a bit funny in her head when the Germans took away her son Silvio. She was always waiting for him to come back, but he never did. His sister Anita was our Sunday school teacher, and I loved to follow her when I went to the farm.

One time, we were sitting under the trees with a group of women, enjoying a pleasant afternoon. Planes came suddenly over us, and soon we heard explosions not too far away. The bombardment had begun. The women threw themselves flat under the trees, screaming and moaning; one of them put her fingers in her ears to stop the awful sound. I sat quietly by my mother, who continued to eat her bread and jam very calmly.

Years later, she told me how scared she was, but she did not want to make a scene to frighten the children more. She just prayed and prayed, and still today I see her as a woman of faith.

The time came when we had to return to Torino, where my mother's midwife was. She had delivered

Lidia and me, and my mother wanted to be close to her at this delivery also.

I remember being on a closed train, with horses on one side and people on the floor on the other side. We had to be very quiet for a while, and all the doors were closed. I was eating a piece of bread, and a man gave me a cookie. I put the cookie between my bread and ate it like a sandwich. I remember being scared of the horses because they were restless.

In Torino we stayed in a small apartment that belonged to friends of ours. The owners were in the country, where they had a cottage, so we could stay at their flat for a while. It was a cold, dank house, and at night we had to cover the windows with blankets so as not to show light on the outside and become a target for the airplanes that bombed the city at all times.

The house had a small stove in the kitchen to keep the whole house warm. It was not often lit because we had no sawdust or other fuel.

Periodically my mother would leave us with a neighbor to go to a place where they sold meat, wood, or other staples. She would line up with other people for a long time, only to be told they had run out of the item, and she would return empty-handed.

Across from our building, there was a factory that had been heavily bombarded. All the windows and doors had been shattered, and, consequently, our doors, which had glass panes, had been shattered. My father hung the blueprints that he brought home from work and every night had to repair the cracks in the panels.

It was a long, very cold winter with lots of snow, and my parents had a hard time keeping us warm and fed, especially my newborn sister, Paola. She was very cute in the blue bonnet that my mother had knitted for her.

My father worked at FIAT, an automobile company, drawing motors parts, and he supplied us with many good things like cookies, jams, and also pieces of fabric. My mother was very skillful in making dresses and slippers for us.

One day in April 1945, we were in my mother's bedroom. She was sick in bed, but the sun was streaming into the room. All of a sudden, we heard bells ringing everywhere. We went to the balcony and saw people hugging, laughing, dancing in the street, shouting that the war was over. The war was really over.

Just as my mother had promised, the Allies had arrived to help us. A new era, when all my dreams would come true, had come. Everything I wanted and asked of my mother would now come, thanks to the Allies.

Little by little, life improved for us. There was more food to be found. We could have things like fruit, cakes, and meat. My parents would come home from the church with all sorts of candies, coffee, sugar, cookies, clothes, and shoes. Wonderful CARE packages began arriving from a faraway place called America. I started to dearly love the Americans who sent us those wonderful things.

One night in the summer, we were at the church. A big party was going on. There were Chinese lanterns hanging from the trees around the garden, and my aunt Pam had made an enormous batch of lemonade punch in a washtub.

There were many American soldiers, the wonderful Allies my mother talked about, and I was so happy to finally see them. Then I saw my sister Lidia and my cousin Emmanuele sitting on the lap of a soldier, eating candies. What about me? I was left out.

I was running in the garden, looking for my father, when a big soldier picked me up. He gave me a bag of peanuts and an O Henry bar. I had never seen anything like it in my life, and I showed those treasures to my dad, who was nearby. He let me eat the chocolate, and I never tasted anything so good in my whole life. Even today when I eat an O Henry bar, I think of the kind soldier that made a little girl so happy. And I have the same deep feeling of gratitude for the American people who helped us so much during a terrible war.

My uncle Leo was a teenager when he found himself taken prisoner by the Germans with other young Italian men. I do not know the exact circumstances because I only heard the story from my mother. Uncle Leo was fifteen then, and one day the Germans took their prisoners to the square of a town near Rome where they kept them. In the square there was a fountain, and the young men started to wash themselves. After a while, Uncle Leo found himself alone in the square.

He started to walk on a road in the country and found that nobody stopped him. He continued to walk for several days until he reached Civitavecchia, where his family lived. It was a day of great joy when his parents saw him back home. Nobody could explain what had happened, and my grandfather always said that God's hand had protected his son from harm and led his son home.

A friend of mine, Michele, was fifteen when he joined the Resistance at Monte Cassino near Rome. He stayed in the monastery of the Monte for a few days, but he was scared of the fight going on. In the night he was able to come down from the mountain, and, hiding during the day, he was able to make his way back to his village, which was in that part of Italy. He walked several nights, and then one evening he came to a farmhouse. He was exhausted and had not eaten in several days, but he had been able to travel without being caught by the Germans.

An old woman appeared at the door of the farmhouse with a gun in her hands. When she saw Michele, she let him in and fed him.

Michele remembers she made spaghetti, and, although it is a common staple in Italy, he had never tasted anything better in his life. He stayed with the old woman for a while, helping her with chores, and then resumed his travel, walking by night and hiding by day.

By then he started to recognize some of the territory. And then one day he realized he had stumbled onto his uncle's fields, next to his father's land. It was a familiar place, and, overjoyed, he walked home. The family had thought him dead and was ecstatic to have him home again.

After the war was over, people realized how difficult it was to rebuild their lives. Many had no work, home, or family left.

I remember a young couple with two children, living in a closet under the stairs of an apartment building. The closet was big enough for a double bed, two chairs, and a small table. Every morning the husband would set up his small table outside the building to repair the shoes of people passing by, keeping an eye on the children while his wife went to different homes to do housework for a bit of money.

At that time many families immigrated to the United States, Canada, or Australia and built new, comfortable lives for themselves and their families.

My eldest sister, Lidia, also has memories of the war in Italy. Here are her recollections:

"My first memories go back to the time when I was five years old. They are very vivid in my mind, even though they were about sixty years ago.

"We were in Torino, and I remember well how I would be woken up by the deep rumble of the planes bombarding the city. It is a noise that I still hear in my head. My father would pick me up in my room, where I was fast asleep, wrapping me in a blanket, and would carry me to the shelter where my mother and my sister, Mirella, were already waiting. The shelter was ugly, small, and dark, and people there talked all the time about death and destruction. My mother would ask them not to talk in front of the children, but rather tell them some fables.

"Then we went to St. Antonino di Susa with Uncle Henry and his family. There were two apartments above the church where Uncle Henry was pastor. In spite of the war and the terror of the planes, we enjoyed a good time there. There was a small garden where I played with my sister, Mirella, and my cousin Emmanuele.

"My dad was still working at FIAT and commuted to Torino every day. One night Uncle Henry and my dad didn't come home until 4:00 a.m., because the train they were on had been shot at.

"When I would hear the alarm, I would run out of the house in terror, to take refuge with my mom and Mirella at a farm near our home.

"My mother was pregnant with my third sister, Paola, and when the time came for my sister to be born, we had to go back to Torino, where the midwife was who had been with her when Mirella and I were born.

"We stayed in the apartment of a friend who lived in the country. I remember when there were bombardments, the windows would break, and dad had to fix them with heavy paper and glue made of flour and water.

"We also had a small stove in the kitchen that my dad would fill with sawdust when he found it in some carpentry shops. He had been able to fill a small closet with sawdust and told my mother to stay there when there were bombardments.

"One morning dad left for work, and the alarm sounded. He made it back in time, and we all sat on my mother's bed while my dad sat by its side, praying.

"After my sister Paola was born, my mother could not go to the shelter anymore. But as soon as the alarm sounded, I would open the door, run downstairs, and go alone to the shelter. I was six then. My mother worried about me, could only take refuge in the sawdust closet with my sisters, Paola and Mirella. She found a neighbor nearby and asked her to keep an eye on me.

"Often the water pipes froze, and my mother would send Mirella and me to the courtyard to gather snow, which she melted on the stove to have water for washing.

"I remember the day of the liberation, the end of the war. It was April 25, 1945. My mother was in bed with a migraine. I went downstairs to look for my friend Adelina, and suddenly there was the sound of bells, ringing ad infinitum"

Lidia told us a tale that made me shake with fear and sickness. She had gone to a small plaza near home to play with some friends, when they saw a truck coming very fast in the plaza, with German soldiers sitting with their bayonets upright. The truck took a curve too fast, and it rolled over. The soldiers were hurt, some by the fall; some had been impaled in the face by their bayonets. Lidia remembers one soldier, blinded, with a bayonet through his eyes. He cried for help, unable to walk, while blood poured down his face. Some of the Italians in the plaza tried to help the soldiers, and one man led the blind soldier to a seat nearby.

It was a great disaster, and Lidia had run home, scared and crying for the hurt soldiers. These memories never pass away.

Lidia also says:" Sixty years later, the most intense memory I have is the terror I felt when there were bombardments, to the point that I would leave my mother and sisters to seek safety. I hope my children and grandchildren never experience anything similar, even though life may not be simple for them."

Milano: Marina and Eugenio

Marina lived near Milano, at Varese, and was not yet born during the war, but she remembers stories told by her family. Her father left the Italian Army and went back home when the army was disbanded. He was supposed to then join the German Army, which was in control of north Italy.

A company doing roadwork hired him, and he got a permit from the German Army to stay home and help repair the roads, which the Germans needed to transport their army. Many Italians did this in order to stay home and not be sent to the front.

However, when the Germans left the town of Varese, he was arrested and charged with being a collaborator. On April 25, 1945, he was put on trial and in fear for his life. Then a big commotion happened in town. The war was over, and people were celebrating. His captors left the police van open, and he was free to leave. He went home, back to his family, and they resumed their lives.

When Marina's aunt got married, she made her wedding gown with the silk of a parachute.

Living in the country provided her family with more food, because the farmers grew their own vegetables and had chickens, rabbits, and other livestock. However, in Milano, nothing was left, and many people suffered bitter hunger.

Eugenio lived in a small village near Milano called Besate. The family had black bread when it could be found, and at school the children talked about white bread as a treat. Eugenio lived with friends and had no problems with food.

He robbed eggs and milk, with other children, from the farmers. His mother commuted from Milano, where she worked, and had to avoid the Germans.

Eugenio's Aunt Rosetta used to give the children shots to prevent them from getting sick and bartered shots for the children for food with the farmers.

On the whole, Eugenio and his sister had a good life in Besate. But at night, looking toward Milano, Eugenio would see the lights of the planes. Then he would see a dome of light coming from the explosions of the bombs in 1942.

Today he and his wife Marina have a good life in their retirement years. They travel and see many beautiful places in the world and enjoy the friendship of many friends and their family. They are happy and their life is much more stable than it was during their younger years during the war.

Belgium: Noel

Noel was nine years old when Hitler invaded Belgium. In 1940, when the Germans came in, the country was very industrial but poor. Rouler was his city, and up to the invasion, the city was full of troops pushed from France to Ostende.

There were many fisher boats to transport citizens to England, although they were not big boats.

The English and French were not particularly nice to the people of Belgium, because they looked at them as collaborators or as being in the way.

The Wermacht, the German guards, were favorable to the civilians. Noel remembers they put him on their motorcycles. In his street, the older people would not come out, but the children did not mind the German guards, and the soldiers gave them candies and chocolates. The children understood the soldiers' language, because the Wermacht were from the lower part of Germany. This happened in 1940. For the children, the Germans were all right. Only when the

Wermacht began fighting and disrupting the factories did things changed. The SS and the Gestapo were not friendly with the Belgians.

In 1942 the SS started to show their real face and shipped all sorts of merchandise from the Belgian factories to Germany. The factory across Noel's street was occupied by the SS, although they did not run the operation. Eventually the children were not allowed to cross the street, while families were supposed to give a room to a German.

When the Germans bombed the railway, the children were sent to the country. Noel was sent to an aunt who had land in the country near Ostende, and there he had a normal life. However, the country soon had to ration food.

When the Germans came, they had a lot of money and bought many things, which they shipped back to Germany. They truly robbed Belgium, and in 1942 the Belgian people had nothing. Many of them were better in the country, but when the farmers killed an animal, one-third of the meat went to the Germans.

In 1944 Noel went to a little school in Kortemark, ten kilometers away. It was scarcely populated. The school was called Marchove, and the Germans evacuated the children, putting them in a different house.

One day a truck with uniformed prisoners came, and they were put in the school. They came from concentration camps.

The Germans were losing the war, so many prisoners were sent to work in Germany. The prisoners looked like skeletons, and the villagers were forbidden to give them food.

There was a monastery not far from the school at which the Germans built a large ramp for launching missiles. It was about a hundred kilometers from England, but a lot of the missiles did not make it. The ramp was found after the war, when the Germans were trying to blow everything up.

One night there was a terrible fire only five kilometers from the road, creating a large crater.

In the school gymnasium, people from nearby houses saw prisoners hanging by their feet and beaten.

When the war was over, the Germans did not want to face what was in the school. They planned to put all remaining prisoners in the school and burn everything down. They were chased away before they could.

Thanks to the great support of the Belgians, some prisoners managed to escape. The majority of Belgian farmers who brought water needed to make concrete for the missile bunker were reported to have belonged to the Resistance.

The prisoners slept on straw, and some died. There were no toilets. Noel was fifteen at this time and could never forget the situation in the school. Still today, when he recounts it, the trauma and emotion he still feels are evident.

A group of prisoners, maybe ten, had escaped and took refuge in a cave nearby, but the Germans found them and shot them. One prisoner stayed in the village after the war. He was a Polish butcher and did very well.

In 1942, when the Germans started to use civilians for labor, they gave the civilians a choice: either be paid or be sent to Germany. Noel's uncle was in his twenties and went underground. One night he went home, and the SS surrounded his house. He jumped from a window upstairs and wasn't seen again until after the war. His aunt got engaged to a Canadian, who took off after Noel's uncle finally reemerged.

Noel feels his life was quite normal, in spite of a few impactful episodes. When the war was over, Noel went back to his mother and saw all the city had been bombed. He joined a group of kids who stole food and cigarettes and sold them at the black market. It seems his parents did not mind. At seventeen he realized he was going the wrong way, so he falsified his passport and joined the conscription army. There he straightened up.

The main impact the war had on Noel was a disruption of a normal life. His father and his mother were sent to a work camp and he had to live with his aunt and uncle. His mother became pregnant and returned to Belgium to have her child, but was sent back to the work camp.

As a result, Noel's brother was placed in an orphanage and Noel had no contact with him until after the war.

Mirella Coacci van der Zyl

Noel is not the type of person that dwells on problems, but rather someone who faces things as they come and moves on. Living through the war may have influenced his way of thinking as he was forced to accept the situation and living with all the changes to his family, including living without his parents and not knowing his brother.

Canada: Libby

Some men in Scot Bay, Nova Scotia, left for the war when Libby was thirteen. She remembers the young men coming home on weekend leave. They were in uniform and always did things together in her small village.

They had great times socializing and dancing. After church they would gather around the pump organ at someone's home and sing. People were always eager to open their houses to the community.

A young man was killed in the war, and Libby was angry that it had happened.

Each family had a ration book filled with tickets that allowed them to purchase only a certain amount of food; for example, they were limited to a pound of sugar per month.

Libby's family had a radio and also got the newspaper, so they had access to news of the war. Of course, Libby was too young to understand it entirely.

In 1942, at eighteen, Libby went to Halifax to train as a nurse. She remembers VE Day in 1945 when the war ended. People were jubilant, with some rioting in downtown Halifax. Her own feelings were of relief and happiness that the war had finally ended.

One day there was an explosion at Bedford Basin Village, an ammunition station, which was felt even in Halifax where Libby was. While working in the hospital, Libby remembers people coming in for shelter. Some of the windows shattered from the explosion. Luckily the explosion did not get worse, but was contained, and there was not too much damage.

In Halifax there was a great movement of people in uniform all the time, wherever one went. Libby was a Christian, but her faith was not as deep then as it is today. She was fortunate to have friends who went with her to services held by a Christian couple, and she met many people in uniform that worshipped there.

Her husband, Ken, whom she met after the war, was only seventeen when he joined the army. He was stationed at Petawawa. His mother was quite upset when she realized he had enlisted. He was mechanically minded and taught soldiers how to drive tanks and other war machines. He taught them to drive without lights at night, as part of the soldiers training. He could also fix anything.

During the war her father had a government job, and Libby believed her family was secure. They had everything they needed, while many families in her small community struggled to put food on their tables. In the small community the women knitted socks for the soldiers, and one woman would provide them to the soldiers.

She completed her nurses' training in Halifax, NS, during the war years. In1945, when victory was proclaimed, she remembers the jubilant celebrations which took place all over the world. She remembers a popular war song of that time:

When the lights go on again, all over the world,
When the boys come home again, all over the world
Then there'll be time for things like wedding bells,
And sweethearts will sing, when the lights go on again
All over the world.

Canada: Jean

Jean's older brother went to war. He was sent to fight in the Korean War for a year and got shrapnel in his arm. When the administration found his medical record, they sent him home. Her other brother went to war three times, and he almost lost an eye.

Jean's mother worked at Firestone, and every time a telegram arrived, she was not home. Jean had to go to tell her mother about the bad news.

Her older brother also fought in Europe during the war. He was moved around many times, and there were months when the family did not know where he was.

In Korea he was sitting in a ditch reading one of Jean's letters when a bomb blew the letter apart. Luckily, he got away with only a few scratches. When he returned home, he was a nervous wreck. He took a job as a bartender in a hotel for three months and then went back to his old job, where he was more comfortable.

Jean's memories are not very clear about what happened to the whole family during the war, but she thinks they were all right. She remembers the different impact of the war on her two brothers. The elder one was never all right after he came home and until he died, he was very unstable in his mind. The younger one was all right and enjoyed his life at home.

Jean thinks the war did not do any good, just looking at the state of many nations today. Lots of people are still at war and suffering and she thinks perhaps we did not learn much from the last war.

Canada: Bob

Bob was five when the war started, and he remembers how food was rationed with tokens and cards. Gasoline was also rationed, and Bob scrounged for scraps of metal to sell for money. His school sold savings bonds. For a book of stamps, he would get a certificate. War bonds were very popular because they supported the war.

Bob and his friends used to play war games with toy guns in a field where there were foxholes. He also had lead figurines of soldiers. When the heads fell off, he would light a match to weld the head back on.

His mother used to drink tea without sugar to save it for his dad. Sugar was rationed, as was butter.

Niagara Falls was deemed a restricted area because of the power station. Security guards were posted on the Welland Canal. Everyone who went overseas was a volunteer, because there was no conscription in Canada.

Bob's uncle was not accepted for the war, and Bob's dad was too old. In this way, his family was quite fortunate not to have to go to war.

Toy Guns

When the war broke out, the family vacation to Minor Bay was cancelled because they could not get gas to go, and there were no buses in Welland at that time.

They could go to the movies for ten cents during the war and watch the news.

People were really patriotic, since most of them were of British descent. Italian farmers and others would come to their house and bring vegetables. There was no animosity against the Italians.

Bob remembers going out to the airport in Welland, where pilots trained. One plane crashed, and the pilot landed up in the field and died.

His family had to have a liquor book to control how much alcohol they bought. Cigarettes were very cheap, and several families shared one meat bone for soup.

When the war was over, they had a parade on the street. The people set a bonfire by lighting a pyramid of wooden barrels to celebrate the end of the war.

England: Margaret

When she was young, Margaret remembers everybody talking about war. At that time, Mussolini was in Abissinia, and the young people would sing a parody about him. The British government was frugal and did not want to send their young people to fight. Chamberlain discussed with Hitler that there would be peace in their time. On September 3, 1939, Chamberlain spoke to the people of England, and in Margaret's house, everyone sat around the radio.

Chamberlain said that, as of 11:00 a.m., England was in a state of war with Germany. It was called the Six Months War, but it lasted six years.

Hitler moved fast in his invasion. Margaret's father commented that Hitler must have a big army to spread in every direction.

In school, they had a mask-day drill. The children were issued gas masks and kept them by their desks. Those masks were like a casket with a pump.

People were instructed to tape their windows. No lights or street lamps were supposed to shine at night. At that time, Margaret was ten years old and won a scholarship to go to high school. She did not have a bicycle to ride the one and a half miles to school. They did not make them anymore, in order to save the metal for the war. There were also very few cars. The only person who had one in Margaret's neighborhood was the doctor.

If you had to go out at night, you were allowed only a small flashlight, and it had to be kept it low. The food was rationed, except for fish and vegetables.

Margaret had to stay in line for meat and would buy only animals with skin on.

Knotty Ash was her village, located outside Liverpool, and it was so old that they still had a blacksmith. They had fourteen miles of dock and were bombarded a lot.

At 8:00 a.m. each day Margaret had to go to the health clinic to check the casualties to see if any of her relatives had died.

Her father could not go to war because he was too old and had epilepsy. One day her paternal house was destroyed. Three days later, they found her grandfather had survived. Sometimes they had to have compulsory evacuees in their house. Margaret's family took in the grandfather, who could not read or write; however, he could pilot a boat. He brought an enormous clock with him into Margaret's house.

When the children came home from school, they wanted a snack. So her grandfather took a bowl of dough from the pantry, slapped it onto their bread, and made them eat the soggy bread. Later on, he went to live with his daughter.

The children did not take war too seriously. If the alarm rang, they had to go to the nearest shelter until it stopped. Then they had to go to school. They were not counted as late, because of the air raid.

They had what was called the Morrison shelter and the Anderson shelter; each family got what they could put together. like food and material to build the shelters.

Schools seemed to be targeted by the Germans, and so the children were separated into groups of ten and sent to different houses for two-hour classes.

The teacher did six hours of teaching a day, in three different homes. Later, a big air-raid shelter was erected on the school grounds.

When a house was destroyed, townspeople would fill the basement with an emergency water supply that would be used to put out fires caused by the next bombing raid.

England: Mary

Mary lived in Upperwood with her grandmother and her aunt. When the sirens rang, they all went under the big table with the dog. Her mother had died in 1940, and then Mary went to live at a convent with her grandmother.

In 1941 Mary was evacuated to southeast London with other schoolchildren, and she was placed with a family she remembers as Auntie Nan and Uncle Tom. There was also a boy named Peter, and they lived right across the street from a school.

Mary sold pop bottles for a penny, and one time, she slipped on the ice and broke both wrists. She must have stayed in that house with Nan and Tom for eighteen months. Once, she was at the train station, and a service man gave her some gum. She remembers the incident, because when she got married, she had gum that tasted exactly like the kind the service man gave her.

Mary was happy with her new London family and did not mind the bombing too much. Eventually, she returned home, but it was too early, as there was still much bombing. There was a lull during her evacuation, but then the Blitz started. When she left for the evacuation, she was allowed only a small case and a gas mask around her neck.

She stayed with her father at his father's house. The sirens would sound, and people went to the air-raid shelters in the gardens until the sirens stopped. Her father used to take her. They went to the shelter with candles, bread, and cheese. The next day, after one raid, she and her father emerged from their shelter and saw all the windows were gone from their house, and the furniture was smashed. Her father sat down among the rubble and said, "I lost my wife, and now I have lost my house."

Mary's grandfather moved to a different house, and her uncle arrived from a prison camp in Singapore. Her uncle did not treat his mother well. The war had made him angry, and he took it out on her. Mary's father remarried in 1945, and Mary went to live with him and his new wife, but it was not a happy relationship. It was a hard time, with rationing and a lack of work.

Her grandmother took her to Sunday school, and she received the Lord in her heart in Baptist Mission Church. Her father blamed God for his wife's death.

Mary remembers the rationing, because she had to stay in line with her book when she was ten, while other children went to the movies.

When she was 20, the family came to North America, California. she thought how plentiful the country was, remembering standing in the long queues with ration books in 1947, for meat, eggs and other items.

In 1983 she emigrated to Canada which was a wonderful chapter in her life.

Thinking back how the evacuation of the children and the War affected her, was a lesson never to forget and taught her to make the most of every situation one might be put and be thankful for our loved ones and for what we have.

England: Ted

Ted was evacuated to his aunt's house in the country with his mother. He has fond memories of happy family times, just being together and enjoying every day. He grew up close to his family, and remembers doing chores for his grandmother. He remembers the V2 rockets and the explosions of the bombs.

His dad told him that they lived on the highest grounds in London. It was called Crystal Palace, where Queen Victoria had the exhibition of the World Fair in 1851, to celebrate the goodness of the Empire Pax Britannica. The exhibition was built in Hyde Park.

During the Blitz some of the bombs fell into the river; their targets were the nearby docks. Ted's father would see the bomb squadron lined up across the river.

Their neighborhood was often targeted for bombing, because it was a popular area.

He sang in the choir of the Anglican Church in Stratford, east London, and remembers hearing the sound of shrapnel raining down on the roof.

Because they lived near the docks, food was easy to come by for his family. Everyone in the neighborhood also maintained victory gardens as a means of increasing food production.

Ted recalls that potassium bombs could not be put out with water, so he dumped a bucket of sand on one.

England: Pat

Pat remembers the noise of the bombers flying overhead when she was only two years old. She and her family had to be rushed to a shelter. The shelters were built for the war, and there they had a sing-a-long. When the "all clear" was given, she could go home, but she was frightened by all that noise and confusion.

She was never hungry. Her mom used to get a sheep's head to make soup. When Pat was four, their neighbor told them he could get half a rabbit for Christmas, and that was the best Christmas they had. They had a coupon book, and every person was allowed two ounces of everything, so they managed to keep the pantry well stocked.

She had clothes because her mom was a machinist. Pat knew she had a dad, but she had not seen him yet, because he was in India with the army. Her mom would sew window leathers for money.

Teenagers went to the factories with the women. The land army girls worked in the fields while the men were gone.

Pat was in Manchester, because children were sent to live in the country with different families for their safety. Pat was too young, so she stayed home with her mom.

When she was five, she met her dad and had chocolate for the first time. Her dad had brought it home for her. He also brought her a dressing gown made out of an army blanket that someone in India had made. Once she got to know her dad, she was very happy he had returned home.

France: Michelle

Michelle remembers that there was little peace in her small village near the coast of France. There were endless convoys of soldiers carrying big machine guns, planes rumbling overhead, and explosions that interrupted her sleep at night. The farm where she lived with her family was relatively safe, and they did not suffer too much, except for the terror she felt when she saw all those soldiers in their big trucks and heard the bombs exploding.

One day it was very sunny and bright, and she was playing in the yard with her dog, Matis, when suddenly one of those big, frightening trucks stopped in their yard. Screaming, she ran to her mother, and then her father joined them with her older brothers. These soldiers were friends, because she heard them speak a bit of French and laugh a lot. Everyone shook hands all around. The word "Allies" was repeated a few times, but Michelle stayed behind her mother the whole time.

Then she saw a black soldier coming toward her. She screamed and ran as fast as she could into the fields. She had never seen anyone with such dark skin so close up and wondered if he was a person like everybody else. She stopped behind a big oak tree and sank down, trying to catch her breath. The soldier had not followed her, and she started to relax a bit.

Michelle must have fallen asleep, because suddenly she heard music and clapping, and then, looking at her house, she saw a big commotion going on. Her father and some neighbors were putting up tables and chairs. People were bringing food: freshly baked bread, salami, and focaccia. Her father and brothers were bringing up bottles of wine from the canteen. She realized a party was going on and slowly made her way back to the farm. She smelled her mother's special rabbit roast, made with small onions, wine, and rosemary, and realized how hungry she was.

The table was full of food from the entire neighborhood: salads, small cakes, ham, vegetables, wine, and many packages of chocolates and candies, which the soldiers had brought. She could not understand why all these festivities were taking place. The neighbors played the accordion and the guitar; her brother played his violin; and people were dancing and clapping. It was a joyous moment.

Then the black soldier approached her, and she trembled, hiding behind her mother, who laughed and told her to look up. Then she saw the dark hands of the soldier holding a box with the most beautiful doll she had ever seen. He was giving it to her, and his smile was the whitest she had ever seen. Hesitantly, she took the doll and made a little curtsy to the soldier. The doll was blonde with a very pretty dress, and she loved it instantly. She thought the soldier was very good to give it to her and said so to her mother, who did her best to relay this to the soldier.

France, Normandy, and Belgium: Chet

Canada's first contribution to World War II was establishing a flying school well away from the fighting zones. The Royal Air Force was rapidly expanding, and Canada was trying to keep manpower at home.

Canadian officers were concerned the Royal Canadian Air Force would become a manning pool if there were no more identified units. Five squadrons that served in Western Europe and the Mediterranean Theatre were formed in 1941 in the United Kingdom. One of these squadrons was 411. Its badge bore a bear, a fierce fighter among the animals of Canada.

The pilots of 411 put their Spitfires to good use during the long months of the war in the skies. They guarded shipping along Britain's east coasts and clashed with the Luftwaffe's Messerschmitts in the skies of France, the Netherlands, and western Germany.

In Belgium they were stationed near Brussels. The civilians were very friendly and did all they could for the Canadians. The people of Holland were also very grateful to see the Canadians.

Chet says that he is glad he went overseas, but he is very glad that his boys did not have to go.

One day in Belgium, Chet and his companions went to a bar, and a man they met there said that he would be like a father to them. He fed them and helped them in every way he could. The Belgians could not do enough for them, and the soldiers felt like Eisenhower. Chet remembers being scared when he flew to England on a DC3 without doors, because it was a plane for airborne infantry. He was also scared when he saw the Germans come. They bombed a place nearby and left a hole as big as a house. At that time, Chet was only twenty years old.

When the war was over, Chet travelled to a prison camp on the border with Germany and saw people dying before his eyes. The Canadians gave the prisoners all the food they had and saw that people had suffered terribly. Children came to take scraps of food from their dumpsters.

In Holland the Canadians were also welcomed. They traded cigarettes for their ham and cheese. Chet traded a pair of boots for a ham once there. At that time, his squadron was on the move. They followed the army.

After the war, many Dutch people came to Canada and Brantford, where Chet now lives. Many Canadians went back to Holland, where their cemetery is well kept, but Chet has not been able to make that journey.

Chet was impatient to get home to marry his lovely girl, waiting for him, but the war went on for a while. When finally he got back, he was married in 1946.

He had lived in a protective family and when he went abroad, he was very sorry to see those horrible things in Europe. He had a sense of relief when the war ended, also for the German soldiers who were able to go back home. However, it was a war that had to be fought to free the people from the Nazi regime.

Germany: Horst

Horst came to Canada in 1976 from Dusbork, north of Dusseldorf, Germany. When the war started, it was also the beginning of Horst's first year in school, 1939. From 1939 to 1945, he attended eleven different schools. Students were transported to different schools whenever the schools were bombarded. His house was partially burned, and his family had to live in the school. The next year they went to Bavaria for eight weeks. When they came back, they had to live in another school.

Because of the constant bombardments in 1943, they went to the eastern part of Germany. During that time, he went to the gymnasium (which is their equivalent of high school).

When the Russians came, they went back to Dusbork in 1945. Horst was twelve and remembers he always had enough to eat. His father was a baker and always had work, until the bread factory was destroyed in 1944. However, the factory was quickly rebuilt, allowing his father to work again.

Horst's worst memories were of the bombardments, which were throughout the war. His mother spoke out against Hitler, and, to save her, his father joined the Nazi Party. A collector came to take money and metal for the war. He was drunk and said to Horst's mother, "I can shoot you right here." The children were there and began screaming, but the collector left without incident because he knew their father.

His father was called by the Nazi Party several times and warned that his wife had to be quiet about her disagreements.

The last week of the war, Horst's family lived in a bunker with five thousand people and no electricity or water. The Americans were out shooting at all times, and the German people could not go out to do their business.

Horst was constantly scared, because ten to twelve people were found shot every morning. He had no idea where their food came from, but it was not good. One time, his mother bought eighty eggs for four people, and they ate boiled eggs for the whole week. His father was too old for the war, so he stayed in the bunker.

They had to leave the bunker when the Americans came and walk thirty-five kilometers to Werden in the Ruha. They were put on a train to Renklin by the Germans for eight days of travelling, attacked by airplanes the entire time. The train stopped in the bush, the passengers run out, and eighty-seven of them died. At the end of the journey the passengers came to a little village, and there they moved into a small school with other refugees. They were fed by local families.

Ten months later, school resumed, and the teachers had to share living quarters with the refugees. One teacher had seven classes, and they were no fun.

Horst attended the school, from 1945 to 1946 and did not learn anything. He had to teach math to seventh graders. When he left school, his parents did not let him go to the gymnasium program because prisoners from Ukraine who had stayed behind were being killed nearby. Horst instead worked on farms for food, which was good for the family. Then he attended a carpentry school for three years and became a carpenter.

From his class of fifty-two students in 1939, only two survived.

Horst believes that war does not achieve any positive results. According to him, World War II was outdated and did not accomplish anything, like the war in Iraq. Terrorists cannot be fought, but we have to give people a good life. He is a pacifist by nature and hates uniforms. At age ten he had to wear a uniform for the Hitler Youth meetings, and he hated it. For many years he never spoke about his experiences, because he thought people would not understand.

Horst feels for the children in Afghanistan and Iraq who fight in the streets today. Once he and his friend watched an airplane explode and saw the pilot's head split open.

One night there was a lot of shooting, and Horst's father came into their home with a Canadian whose plane had been shot down. "Give me your pistol," his father said to the Canadian, showing him to the basement where others were hiding. Someone asked, "Why did you not shoot him now?"

Horst's father answered, "Because I believe in the Geneva Convention. He is my prisoner, and I will protect him."

Toy Guns

Open trucks travelled in eastern Germany, and some were full of wounded soldiers. Horst and his family travelled for two days and two nights back to Dusbork on a train with broken windows and lots of people packed in like sardines. Then they knew that the war was over.

Holland: Rita and Ton

Rita and Ton came to Canada in 1957 and settled in Brampton. When the war started in Europe, Ton was five, and Rita was only two.

In Holland, their family did not have enough food, and so Rita and Ton would go to the common kitchen with a small pan and a spoon three times a week to be fed. The kitchen had thick soup, and they considered it a good meal.

Rita's father was a superintendent at the bank, which was housed in a five-story building. After their first house was bombed, her family moved to an apartment upstairs from the bank. They knew everybody in the building. The bank was never bombed.

Rita was never afraid, even when the alarms sounded. Her family would go to the basement with their pillows; her mother and father sat trembling, but the bombs never hit them.

One day they were going to the dentist, which was located in the middle of their building, and they walked past two Dutch soldiers who had been shot near a shelter.

They had to hang thick, black paper on the windows and made lamps out of aluminum pots; the fuel was carbide, which stank. They were always afraid that the lamps would explode.

Ton remembers standing behind the curtains in 1940, watching antiaircraft fire shooting at the airplanes as they approached Rotterdam. His father cried at the sight of Rotterdam in flames. In 1941 his family went to the country to live in a house built on a dike. The dikes were bombarded, and their basement was completely flooded. They filled the basement with cinder blocks so they could walk there.

The boys went out on their bikes and insulted the Germans. The Germans had their headquarters in the building where Ton's father worked. There was a cannon on the roof, and one day a German picked Ton up and dangled him from the rooftop, but did not drop him.

When lightning once hit and knocked over a pole, killing a German soldier, the people in the area were blamed for killing him. Seven houses were set on fire, and the men there were taken out and shot. The German commandant wanted to burn down all the houses on the dikes for three kilometers, but his superiors stopped him.

Ton's dad used to cross the bridge to get eggs and spiced vinegar. He would give the eggs to the Germans guarding the bridge and then go across and get some bread. Then he would reverse the procedure and come home with a suitcase full of bread.

Rita says that the memories of being hungry never leave her, so she never throws away anything and recycles everything. She never throws food out.

At the times of harvest, the farmers would let Ton help and take home some of the bounty to his mother, who used to make porridge out of it.

At night, Rita would go to the attic and watch out of a little window where she would see young men being rounded up and put onto trucks. The Germans took them away to Germany, and she would hear their cries. She still loathes being alone at night in her house.

The V2 rockets would pass over Ton's family's house, and they would see them overhead as they made their way to where the Allies were stationed. The Allies would then shoot them down.

One time they heard that the Allies were going to bomb Germany. The Germans would drop empty fuel tanks, but one time one dropped with gas still in it. Ton and his brother went with a bottle to collect the fuel. The Germans took his brother, keeping him for three days.

The sound of sirens still frightens Ton. He once saw a fight between a Spitfire and a Messerschmitt.

In 1944, the Danish Air Force flew overhead, dropping packages of food. People fought in the fields over the parcels. Rita will never forget the taste of that bread.

Both Rita and Ton still feel the impact of the war today. They travelled to Europe this Spring and visited the famous Auschwitz camp. Rita had tears in her eyes as she tells us, her friends in Canada, how the memories of those horrible events flooded her mind and overwhelmed her, even though she was not in any camp. She and Ton pray constantly for the well being of the world and for peace among the nations.

Holland: Betty

Betty remembers the planes flying overhead while her family hid in cement bunkers in 1940. She was nine years old. Her family lived in a farmhouse in Holland, and Betty remembers that the Germans came and told them to leave their house because they wanted to convert it into a hospital.

They moved to a horrible little house where the water would conduct electricity. Betty's sister was two years old, and the German soldiers used to put her on their shoulders, march her around, and give her food from their canteens. The soldiers burnt the family's Dutch flag and books in the fields.

Her father used to grow fruit in their greenhouse, and one time, someone had rigged the floor, which exploded, throwing her father up into the air. He was okay; the soldiers just wanted to bug him. However, Betty's mother was shaking like a leaf. The soldiers then threw all the furniture out of the house. They had no mercy.

Betty remembers that people came from the city to the country to look for food. Her mother made bread from sugar beets and wheat picked up from the ground that the miller ground for her. One day they would eat potatoes, and the next day they would eat the peels. This was how they were able to survive.

Neighbors would get up in the middle of the night wearing black clothes and kill a farm animal to feed their family.

Betty's mother was pregnant but adopted a child who was always crying because starvation had ruined his body.

One time the German soldiers poured gasoline on the fruit her father grew, ruining it and taking away the income that came from it.

After the war, some of the young Germans dated Dutch girls, and the Dutch people shaved the girls' heads for fraternizing with the enemy. Betty's cousin was one such girl.

There was no school left, because the Germans had taken them all over. The school board was able to get barns with outhouses, and the children could go to school for just a few hours a day for each grade. After fifth grade, Betty could not go to school anymore and had to help her mother around the house. Her mother had suffered a miscarriage. Later on, when her mother had another baby, Betty looked after him, and he became her little guy.

Betty used to walk to the village to stand in line for soup, and after waiting a long time, all she got was a watery broth with a few pieces of meat and vegetables.

In 1951, her family came to Canada. Betty did not want to leave Holland because she was seventeen and by this time, she had a job. She also had to leave her bicycle behind, which made her very sorry. On the boat from Holland, she met her future husband.

The family settled in a poor house, where they could see the sky from inside and they had to use a lot of buckets when it rained. But they had to make the best of it, because her father had lost everything in Holland when the Germans had poured gasoline on his fruit trees and nothing could grow anymore.

Toy Guns

Eventually, they moved to Boston where her father worked in an orchard and her future husband could come to court her. Then they were married And had a good life in Canada.

Holland: Sylvia

Sylvia's father was a pioneer of the northeast polders. These were dikes built to keep the land from the sea. There were Germans in the village at the time. These soldiers were elderly and treated the villagers better than other soldiers in Holland. They went underwater to save the boys from being taken to the front. Sylvia's two brothers, who were nineteen and twenty-one, were taken into hiding.

The family lived in a boathouse. Three weeks before the war was over, the SS came to remove them from their house, because they needed it for an office, but they did not take their boat.

Sylvia heard the drone of the planes overhead; there was war above them. Her mother used to collect the bullets that fell from the planes. One plane crashed near their house, but the pilot was safe, and they took him in.

One day, when she was in school, a fight broke out amongst the soldiers, and they burned two farms. The principal took Sylvia to see it.

Toy Guns

In 1999, Sylvia went back to Holland. She and her family were standing on the grounds of their old house when two big planes flew very low over them. Sylvia was instantly brought back to memories of the war.

One time they were eating lunch in a bungalow when sirens went off. It was a test to see that the sirens worked well.

Some people had hidden a few boys on their farm; one of them was hidden in the trunk of a car. The lady of the house told the soldiers to look in the trunk, but they did not believe her and did not look there, so in that way she saved his life.

When she was a child, Sylvia had a difficult time keeping her mouth shut. Her mother always told her not to answer the soldiers who asked questions. As a result, she became very shy.

Her uncle once said, "Oh, Hitler is no good," and was heard. So the SS took him to a concentration camp until the war ended. The Jews in their village left, and they were never seen again.

There was very little fighting where she lived. The day of liberation, her family went to church and wore blue and orange, the colors of Holland, on their coats. They were told to go home and hide their possessions, because the SS were coming back. The Germans bombed the Friesland, injuring or killing many people.

 Eventually Canadian soldiers arrived in tanks and gave the children candies and chocolate. The elderly German soldiers gave themselves up. They were friendly with the Canadians because they had not wanted the war.

Java: Theo

Recently, in the Netherlands, there was a commemoration of the Battle of the Java Sea, which took place in 1942. At this ceremony, the son of Rear Admiral Dorman, Theo, spoke about what he remembered from those days.

He recounted his experiences during the war:

I was six years old, and just like many European boys my age I had a magnificent childhood in the Netherland East Indies. With my father and my mother, his second wife, we lived on Java street in Subaraya. When my father was at sea, my mother and I stayed in Pacet, in the mountains above Subaraya.

Then the war broke out. My father's bed was reinforced and placed on blocks in order for us to crawl underneath it during air raids. I was given a British helmet, a bag with a nameplate, a blood group certificate, and some filthy-tasting India rubber to bite during bombardments.

At the beginning of February, the bombing of Surabaya began. Toward the end of February, two ships, the *Ruyter* and the *Java*, sailed into Surabaya after a night operation in the Bandung Strait between Bali and Lombok. The *Piet Hein* had been sunk, and the *Tromp* was badly damaged.

My mother and I came back to Java Street from the mountains. My father was kept busy dealing with the commanders of the ships for the next operation, repairing the damage that had been done, concern for the wounded and casualties from the *Tromp*, and the collection of survivors from the *Piet Hein*.

As the *Tromp* departed for Australia, my father said to his commander, "Jan, you still have a chance, but we will not see each other again." Although I did not realize it at the time, he was leaving us forever, and we were brought back to the mountains.

The telephones were cut off, and late that afternoon my mother heard from one of our neighbors that a violent battle with the Japanese had taken place and that the *DE Ruyter* and the *Java* had been sunk.

We immediately drove to Surabaya and slept that night on mattresses on the ground at an acquaintance's house, because our house was not considered safe. The following morning my mother told me that I would probably not see my father again. She went by bicycle to the navy commander, who advised her to get ready for evacuation to Australia. The next morning we received instructions to report to the Goebeng barracks within the hour with one suitcase.

Toward the end of the afternoon, we arrived at a flooded piece of land where four Catalina flying boats lay waiting with their tails over the riverbank. After some problems starting the engine, we were the last who were able to climb into the jam-packed flying boat as night quickly descended on us. The windows were blacked out, and the crew was able to prepare a pot of warm pea soup.

Suddenly machine guns sounded in the darkness, but fortunately that was just to test the weapons. And so we flew into the night and landed the following morning near the town of Broome, approximately six hundred kilometers south of Timor.

Java: Dan

Dan's father was in the army in Mangalang as a sergeant. The Japanese came, and Dan's family was sent to a concentration camp in Ambarana as prisoners of war. Dan was ten year old. He was sent to Jakarta and Tiateng. Then he was sent to a youth camp near Bandung. The camp was formed to prevent young boys from forming an army and creating problems for the Japanese. Today, Dan still speaks Malay.

Life in the camp was boring and terrible. Dan had a dog there, but not for long. Food consisted of rice with some vegetables, hardly any meat, and no fruit.

His mother and sisters ended up in Batavia, and his mother did the laundry for the Japanese.

The boys were not in shape to play, because they all suffered from malnutrition. Dan looked older than his age.

After he came out of the camp, the locals strapped a Grenade to his knees because he was Dutch.

When the war was over, he joined his mother and sisters in Jakarta, where his family enjoyed a bit more food. Soon after, the family went back to Holland on the Ryndam, where they lived in an emergency shelter and then a house with a dirt floor until they could acquire something better. It was very cold, and Dan's sister had pants made of curtains.

Dan went to school in 1946 when he was about thirteen years old, continuing on to high school.

In 1997 Dan went back to Indonesia to pay respect to his father's grave, and there he picked up a severe bug, losing fifteen pounds. The last ten years have been difficult for Dan, as sickness has affected his memory and malnutrition from the camp has caught up with him.

It is still not safe in Indonesia today. To some extent the Dutch people exploited and abused the locals for three hundred years, so even after the war, the Dutch were not liked.

Scotland: Lin

Lin was six when she was living in Ballouch, Scotland. On a hill, she could see the German planes bombing the shipyards. The bombers always flew over town. She saw a plane land near their house, and the pilot was very young, not even eighteen.

The Germans flew over the school and dropped a bomb, which never exploded. It was an act of God, according to Lin.

Her brother joined the navy when he was sixteen and was stationed outside Naples. He was on a reserve tugboat, when he saw the terrifying image of an exploding ship, its crew in the water surrounded by burning oil. Even today he still has nightmares about that event. The buzz bombs were the worst, the silent killer the sailors heard in the afternoons.

In Scotland, when the sirens sounded, everybody had to go to the shelter. Lin remembers how her dog, Ben, would touch her face when she was sleeping to edge her out of bed to go to the shelter. He seemed to sense when the bombers were coming and stayed with Lin until all was clear. He was a sheepdog and had the instinct of herding her to safety.

Till today, Lin thinks that dogs can be the best friends of people and save them with their lives.

Singapore and Holland: Nellie

Nellie was born in Singapore, where her father worked for the Shell Oil Company. In 1938 her family came to Holland, while her aunt, who was in Sumatra, ended up in a Japanese camp.

Nellie and her family landed in Hilversum during the Nazi occupation. There were four children in the family.

They had a large house, and in 1943 things began to change. Her parents could not buy clothes in the store for the new baby they had. There was no electricity, no water, and no gas. There was no soap either, and their hands were raw from washing without it.

They were asleep one morning when they heard that war had started with the Germans. Workers had to leave their offices for the Germans.

At the beginning of the war, stores were filled with anything people wanted, but as time went by, goods became scarce. Some days stores had only potatoes and cabbages. In 1944 Nellie's family had some meat and potatoes, but the next day they only had one loaf of bread. They ate soup from the central kitchen that tasted like dirty water. There was a barter system for getting food, and Nellie's mother went to the city hall to acquire some.

In the mornings, her father got up at five to have a bath and then left the tub filled for the rest of the family.

The girls grew older, and their mother reused their clothes for the younger children. It was more difficult to clothe boys. Nellie's brother had only one pair of pants, and one day he came home with a piece missing. His mother sent him out to look for it, because she could patch it back up. Despite the scarcities, they felt that God was present and participated in their lives.

One Sunday morning, the square was full of Germans.

Nellie's father stored his potatoes on the veranda, but it was very cold, so one of his friends who had a truck picked them up and kept them in his barn. People were very hospitable and helped each other. Nellie's was a close family. In those days the motto was "With Germany there is freedom all over the world."

Not all Germans were Nazis. People on the other side could not condemn the whole nation of Germany. The Nazis were searching all the houses for food and other goods they could use.

Many people harbored Jews in their homes. At one time, when Nellie was nine years old, her family hid a Jewish woman in the house, and it was very dangerous. This woman was in her forties and had no ID. They gave her a room upstairs in their house, but she could not go outside for three months. Nellie's father talked to his children and told them not to say a word about their guest to anybody. After three months, the Jewish woman was able to move freely around the house and help Nellie's mother with the new baby. Still, they had to be on guard all the time.

Nellie remembers singing Christmas carols when they heard the drone of planes. Then a bomb exploded near their house. She also remembers standing in line with her sister for food and coming home with two and a half loaves of bread. Her mother made porridge with barley, and someone gave them anchovy water. They placed it on the stove and as it heated, it separated, and they were then able to put salt on their porridge.

In the bush, they found grass that was like salad. After the war, no cats or dogs could be found in the streets. Children died in the street for starvation. One night all the trees around Nellie's house were cut down, but the family had not heard a thing.

Today Nellie is retired in a comfortable cottage by a lovely pond where she can hear the bird songs and walk to her church, which is a short distance away. She is at peace and feels safe.

Uganda: Rick

Although he never experienced the trauma of war firsthand, Rick Gamble, a reporter with the *Brantford Expositor*, went on assignment to the war-torn country of Uganda. His stories are about the child soldiers who came in the night, to rape, murder, and mutilate villagers. Here are his notes relating the experience:

Stella was kidnapped by rebels at fourteen and kept in the bush. She was tasked with torturing others who were captured in their raids. Then she returned home. She, along with others, took children and marched a long time. When their prisoners got tired, they were killed.

Stella and her brother were digging in the fields, and she asked him, "Do you want to rest?"

"Yes," he said. Stella took her hoe and killed him, and then she cut the body into pieces and left him in the garden.

She went back to the rebels and led them to her parents' home, which she looted and then burned.

Eventually she went back home and asked her parents for forgiveness for killing her brother, and they forgave her. Stella was so brainwashed by the rebels that whenever she saw a farming tool, in her mind she saw it as instrument of war.

Stella received counseling and forgiveness, and now she wants to study to become nurse, because she killed so many people. She wants to heal people, not kill them.

Many of these former child soldiers want to be doctors, nurses, or teachers to atone for the atrocities they committed. They want to do something to merit their own forgiveness.

The villagers welcomed back their children when the war was over. These children went back to the villages where they murdered, raped, and looted. They are accepted because the villagers knew them and also knew that they were forced to commit those atrocities, or else they would have been killed.

These children are plagued by nightmares of the people they killed. For the rest of their lives, they cannot escape these memories. They are also ready to forgive their captors, those people who stole their childhood. They do that mainly because it gives them peace, which is important to them.

In Uganda, Christianity is the dominant religion, and most people have a personal belief in Christ. Their faith compels them to forgive. Most of the people who come out of the bush do not go back to their old lives. Child soldiers find ways to rebuild their lives.

The Catholic, Muslim, and Anglican Churches worked together to lobby for peace and reconciliation.

The rebels kidnap children as young as ten years old because they are easy to terrify, and then they send the children home to kill their parents. After they kill one person, they are forced to be one of the rebels.

It happens that if the rebels see a person on a bicycle, they will mutilate his leg so he is unable to get away.

The rebels call themselves the Lord's Resistance Army. They say they want to rule Uganda using the Ten Commandments, distorting the words of the Scripture to justify their conduct.

A cease fire has held now for ten years. People have gathered in internally displaced camps, truly refugee camps, where people live in huts and are protected by the government, although they do a very poor job of it.

The children band together in support groups to find love and support in each other. When life is so fragile, it becomes either very precious or cheap to a child soldier. Those who have experienced this fragility take nothing for granted. Forgiveness is noble and necessary, because without it, we become prisoners of our actions.

Vietnam: Bill

Bill was twenty-one when he was conscripted into the US Army. He was with the ROTC (Reserve Officers' Training Corp) for ten weeks of basic training and skills assessment in South Carolina. He received his commission as a mathematician and then went to Port Sill, Oklahoma, where he was trained as a fire direction officer.

Bill was a second lieutenant and spent eight months learning how to fire rockets. Then he went on leave, and when he returned, his unit was deployed to Vietnam. Soon he was on a transport ship and then landing in Quinon, where he was assigned to Pleiku.

He stayed in the highlands for two months and learned how to use the artillery.

Then they moved to the central part of Vietnam, where they were artillery support for the main force and security support for the area. Often they were called on to fire artillery at night, because the Viet Cong would conduct patrols at that time.

The area held traps constructed of bamboo with sharp tips dipped in feces, causing any wounds they inflicted to become infected.

As fire directions officer, Bill rode in helicopters a lot and relayed instructions to soldiers on the ground as to where to direct their artillery. He lost twenty-one men, all eighteen- and nineteen-year-olds.

For him it was just a job, because he was not confronting his enemy face-to-face. Often, when the Viet Cong came too close, he would call in an air strike of Napalm bombs.

In 1966 a car of monks set themselves on fire to protest the war.

When Bill went home, he was decommissioned and, as inactive reservist, could have been recalled anywhere for up to four years later. He wasn't called "and was eventually discharged.

Vietnam: Kim

In 1992 Kim Phuc came to Canada. As an adult, she has started to tell her story of war from when she was a young girl in Vietnam. She allowed us to take notes during her talk and to publish them.

She remembers a happy childhood. She lived in a very nice house in Vietnam and felt safe. Before the war forty-nine years ago, she was never afraid of anything. Then one day soldiers pounded on her door; it was the first time that she experienced fear. A Napalm bomb fell on her village, and she remembers running with other children through the village.

There is a famous picture of her running naked through the village, with the smoke of the bomb behind her. The photo has been printed in many magazines. It helped the world see the war in a different way. The photographer who took the picture was the one who rushed Kim to the hospital.

Reflecting on what she learned from her war experience, Kim said she learned to be strong at nine years old. Three days after she had been brought to the hospital, she was left to die. She had been burnt all over her back and arms, and the pain was unbelievable. She stayed in the hospital for fourteen months and had seventeen operations. Somehow she found the strength to live.

In 1994 a final operation gave her the freedom to move her neck. At times the pain comes back like a knife, so she distracts herself and never concentrates on it. She is a Christian and says that prayer helps her a lot.

As a child she discovered the importance of love and of working together. Kim does not forget the compassion of her doctors and the help her family gave her. Her skin was always tight and itchy, and sometimes she felt sorry for herself. Touching her scars on her arms and on her back, she always thought, *Why me? I will never get married or have a baby. Love is not always easy and gentle.*

Kim's mother would tell her how much she loved her, but she could not take away Kim's pain. Kim was the one who had to endure it, especially when she did her physical therapy exercises.

Her family's house in Vietnam was destroyed. They had nothing left, but the family worked together to stay alive.

When she got better, the first thing Kim wanted to do was go back to school. She wanted to be a doctor because she had been in the hospital so long and had seen what the good doctors did. She entered medical school. However, the government tried to control her.

Kim wanted to live a peaceful live, but she was not allowed to be free. When she was not free in 1982 from the government control, it was a low point in her life, and she wanted to die. She hated her life and anyone who was normal. She was angry and bitter.

In 1986, the government sent her to Cuba, though her health was not good. There she had to learn Spanish.

It was while she was in Cuba that she learned to love God, and eventually she found Jesus. She spent many days in the library studying, and then she found the Bible. She went to church, where she heard and could talk about Jesus. Finally she made her peace, and in 1992 she accepted Jesus in her heart.

She thanked God for giving her a new faith. From then on she chose to live, to move on and help others.

The government was always watching her. They assigned a woman to watch Kim twenty-four hours a day. In 1986, in Cuba, Kim finally had the chance to escape from that oppression. She had not understood why she had to stay so long in Cuba, but there she met a man and married him.

She and her husband defected to Canada, and they have known freedom ever since.

To forgive those who caused her great suffering was a big challenge for Kim. It seemed impossible; she was only human. But she was determined to learn to forgive. She had to stop asking, *Why me?* In Jeremiah 3:3 she found to phrase, "Call upon me," and it was her number. From her faith, she learned to be confident.

It is an amazing miracle that the little girl from that famous photo of long ago is still alive today and can speak of her experiences. She now has three honorary degrees as a doctor.

Epilogue: The War within Ourselves

As I interviewed people about their memories of war, they all expressed a reaction. Some had tears in their eyes; some were angry; some were careful about what they said.

They all suffered through the war during their childhood, and many of them still carry the impact of those conflicts as adults.

Many are very frugal in their lifestyle and careful with their possessions. Living through war taught them that they may lose everything and that the future may not be secure. They have to call on their ability to restore, repair, barter, and rely only on themselves.

Though the wars these people lived through are over, another kind of war still rages inside many of them. This inner war is more insidious, because it keeps them from being at peace. This inner war manifests itself in many ways: it may be noticed outside our spirit or it may be kept hidden within us. It may ruin our lives if not acknowledged and dealt with.

Toy Guns

Anthony was a member of the church where my father was the minister. It was a small church by the sea in south Italy. My father befriended this man, who was seeking peace within himself. He had a very volatile temperament and used to beat his wife and children if they did not obey him. One time he even ran after his wife with a gun. When his temper rose, he would sometimes smash what little furniture they had in their small house. Clearly he was at war with the world.

He knew he had a problem and had many talks with my father, because he wanted to change his behavior.

I do not know what the two men said to each other. I just remember Anthony coming to my father's study many times at night, where they talked and prayed.

Eventually his inner war subsided. He became a new man, and one of his neighbors remarked that the change was so remarkable he wanted to know Anthony's secret.

There came a happy time for all of us when he confessed to the whole church that Christ had changed him and he wanted to be baptized.

Anthony showed a loving side to his children when he took them to church for Sunday school. He would line all nine of them up and give them each a small coin to place on the offering plate.

He became my Sunday school teacher when I was a teenager. He had studied the Bible extensively with my father and wanted to pass on what he had learned. I remember him telling us of his love for the Scripture, and especially for the apostle Paul because of the many similarities in their lives. He too had persecuted Jesus with his hot behavior, taking it out on his family and friends.

The war was over in his life, and Christ had won.

For Marie Rosa, the war within was a quiet one.

A group of people gathered on the beach to watch an unusual event take place. The sun was setting. The sea in this part of northern Italy was calm and intensely blue.

Some young people were being baptized in the Tyrrhenian Sea by a group of Baptist believers. Two men were in the water, while a group of young people, dressed in white, waited on the beach. One by one, the young people came to the men in the water, who immersed the youths gently in the sea, while the congregation on the beach sang a hymn.

A girl of sixteen watched the event with tears in her eyes. It was a touching event she was witnessing—the proclamation of one's faith in Christ.

It must have been like this at the time of John the Baptist when he baptized Jesus Christ, she thought reverently. *I want to do this one day and proclaim my faith in Christ*, she decided.

Marie Rosa had not been happy in her life. Her parents were very severe and patriarchal. She had to do what she was told, or else she was not welcome in the house.

But one thing she was firm about was that she would not attend church. The fact that her parents went to church and then were so stern with their children did not sit well with her. They gave her the freedom to choose, but she struggled to reconcile her deep instinct to follow God with her rebelliousness toward the teaching of her family and the Church.

This inner struggle went on for a year, and she knew she had many religious friends who were concerned about her. Those months were sad and empty for her. She did not want to face the issue, but she knew it was there and had to be addressed.

That moment on the beach brought it to a climax. The struggle came to an end almost by itself. She was touched by the demonstration of faith of those young people and realized her ardent wish to be like them. She let go of her rebellion and stubbornness and opened her heart to a new life in faith. She decided to follow Christ for the rest of her life.

She grappled often with thoughts of what would happen if she surrendered to God and spent long nights thinking, *If I die now, what happens to God? Where do I go? Is it all finished?*

Her life had not been pleasant or peaceful, and she longed to end the turmoil but did not have the incentive or spiritual energy to do it.

Now a new life of happiness and serenity had begun, and joy had entered her life.

Ernest did not have a special conversion experience:

I liken the beginning of a Christian life to the dawn of a new day. The sunrises are spectacular in color and brightness. The dawn of my life as a Christian was not noteworthy, except that, from my point of view, it was a miracle that God reached down into my goings on. People in the church that I attended in Halifax, young and old, had been praying for me, for another miracle.

June 30, 1963, I became a Christian and was baptized January 1964, much to the chagrin of my stepfather. He believed in God, and that was the extent of his religion. He was resentful for the loss of his own son during the war. Despite his obvious disappointment, he did not criticize my involvement with the church.

It never occurred to me that there was something missing in my life. I was living at home with my family in Halifax, Nova Scotia, and held a job. My life was uneventful, but it was not unhappy on the whole. It was moderately challenging. I had to be punctual at work and held some responsibilities.

My family never went to church, unless for special events like a wedding or a funeral. During my time at work, I was sometimes sent out to get lunch for the other employees. One of these times, I ran into a former schoolmate, and she casually asked me what my religion was. My mother had told me that if and when someone asked me such a question, I had to reply that I was a Baptist, which was not the case. Apparently she approved of the Baptist beliefs. The matter of salvation, most important in Baptist beliefs, was not impressed on her.

The former schoolmate was happily surprised, because she was of the same persuasion. She invited me to her youth group in one of the largest churches in the city. I was intrigued by what went on during those Tuesday night meetings. Young people, from teenagers to mid-ies, high school students, college and university students, and young working people attended.

After my first time, I never missed a meeting and soon was inducted into the group of those responsible for planning the meetings. I became the treasurer, taking up and banking the weekly offerings.

Often there were retreats and Bible studies, and my faith, ever so slowly but firmly, grew.

Unfortunately, university education at Acadia University beckoned me, and for a while I stopped attending the youth group. On campus we had church-oriented activities, including Bible studies in the Student Christian Movement.

My life became complicated with studying and a new romantic involvement. I was allowed to sit in on lectures for advanced naturalists. My attendance at Acadia only lasted two years. I went to Ontario for a job, which lasted six months, in Algonquin Park as an assistant naturalist.

My life changed, because when I was still in Halifax, I did not sit at home on Sundays but instead went to church three times that day. Tuesdays I attended youth group meeting, and Thursdays were the meetings for the executives to plan the other meetings. Many times we had field trips on Saturdays with a naturalist group I had become interested in. These field trips boosted my faith in God and his creative power.

Later on my faith was the cornerstone of my marriage and in raising my children. I have three children, and they all attended Sunday school. I am disappointed that my children, now that they are grown up, do not attend church.

Nevertheless, my faith in God and in Jesus as my Savior continues to grow, despite all the tragedies and setbacks in my life, and I am thankful to God for leading me on.

War is an unfortunate aspect of human life. For one reason or another, there has always been one group of people that dislikes another to the point of resorting to violence to eliminate the other group. Hatred, intolerance, and fear grow and grow, escalating to, and then beyond, the brink of war. Inevitably, children grow up amidst these conflicts and are affected by them. Some do not act; others hear the call of war and become participants. For other children, war rages within them as they grow up and learn that the world around them is not always peaceful but rather a place that is witness to battles between good and evil, a war over ideologies.

Toy Guns

Children used to play with toy guns made out of plastic, role-playing scenarios of death and violence. This gave way to video games with the objective to destroy onscreen opponents.

In our world today we see countries where war, hatred, and killing rage seemingly without end. Children are used to fight in these conflicts, given a gun they do not even know how to use.

Child soldiers are all too common, brainwashed to take part in civil war and kill their own families. I rejoice when I see kids playing hockey in the streets, skating, or swimming in pools. Those are memories they will keep of harmless games they will continue to enjoy as they grow up, innocent of war.

Will there ever be an end to war, or will war lead to the end of ourselves?

God created all of us and watches over us. He touches our hearts with love and care. In his world, there are still millions of people with the seal of his love on their hearts. We are his children, and we should try to cooperate in keeping this world safe and healthy, especially for our children.

CPSIA information can be obtained at www.ICGtesting.com
Printed in the USA
LVOW07s0513291014

410925LV00002B/8/P